Bunny, Bunny

Bunny, Bunny

Written by Kirsten Hall
Illustrated by Kathy Wilburn

My First
READER

children's press ®

A Division of Scholastic Inc.
New York Toronto London Auckland Sydney
Mexico City New Delhi Hong Kong
Danbury, Connecticut

Library of Congress Cataloging-in-Publication Data

Hall, Kirsten.
   Bunny, bunny / written by Kirsten Hall; illustrated by Kathy
Wilburn.– 1st American ed.
        p. cm. – (My first reader)
Summary: Depicts, in rhyming text and illustrations, the activities of a
bunny playing in the sun.
   ISBN 0-516-22923-0 (lib. bdg.)   0-516-24625-9 (pbk.)
   [1. Rabbits–Fiction. 2. Play–Fiction.] I. Wilburn, Kathy, ill. II.
Title. III. Series.
   PZ7.H1457Bu 2003
   [E]–dc21
                                    2003003609

Text © 1990 Nancy Hall, Inc.
Illustrations © 1990 Kathy Wilburn
Published in 2003 by Children's Press
A Division of Scholastic Inc.

1 2 3 4 5 6 7 8 9 10 R 12 11 10 09 08 07 06 05 04 03

Note to Parents and Teachers

Once a reader can recognize and identify the 24 words
used to tell this story, he or she will be able to read successfully
the entire book. These 24 words are repeated throughout the story,
so that young readers will be able to easily recognize
the words and understand their meaning.

The 24 words used in this book are:

a	fun	on
and	furry	soft
as	having	sun
bunny	his	the
day	hopping	thumping
ends	hurry	tired
friends	in	way
from	now	with

Bunny, bunny,

soft and furry.

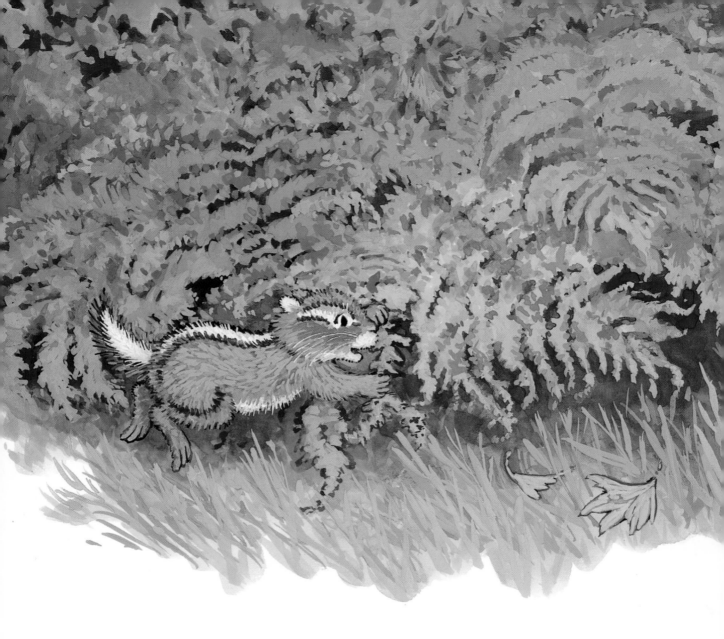

Bunny, bunny,

in a hurry.

Bunny, bunny,

having fun.

Hopping,

thumping,

in the sun.

Hopping,

thumping,

with his friends.

Hopping as the

day now ends.

Tired bunny

on his way.

Tired from

his bunny day!

ABOUT THE AUTHOR

Kirsten Hall has lived most of her life in New York City. While she was still in high school, she published her first book for children, *Bunny, Bunny*. Since then, she has written and published more than sixty children's books. A former early education teacher, Kirsten currently works as a children's book editor.

ABOUT THE ILLUSTRATOR

Kathy Wilburn grew up in Kansas City, Missouri, where she began her artistic career with Hallmark Cards after graduating from the Rhode Island School of Design. She currently lives in Portland, Oregon, where she works as a children's book illustrator.